TRUE-LIFE TREASURE HUNTS

Did you know that…

The pirate Blackbeard is said to have hidden his gold in many places—and wherever he buried treasure he buried a headless skeleton, too!

A man walking on a beach in Florida turned up one old silver coin and then went on to find a fortune in treasure from seven sunken ships!

There's a sunken treasure train in an Ohio river with two million dollars in gold on board!

Judy Donnelly has dug up a wealth of amazing facts about true-life treasure hunts in this entertaining and carefully researched book.

True-life TREASURE HUNTS

Special Book Club Edition

by Judy Donnelly

illustrated with drawings by Charles Robinson
and black and white photographs

SCHOLASTIC INC.

New York Toronto London Auckland Sydney

ISBN 0-590-40230-7

Photo credits: 10, The Bettmann Archive; 13, 17,
22, 23, 26, Robert Marx; 29, Taylor and Dull, courtesy
of Sotheby Parke Bernet, Inc.; 35, Griffith Institute,
Ashmolean Museum, Oxford; 38, 39, 40, 41, 43, 45,
Photography by Egyptian Expedition, The Metropolitan
Museum of Art; 50, Missouri Historical Society; 52, 53,
Wide World Photos.

All rights reserved. Published by Scholastic Inc.,
730 Broadway, New York, NY 10003,
by arrangement with Random House, Inc.

12 11 10 9 8 7 6 5 4   5/9

Printed in the U.S.A   40

First Scholastic printing, February 1987

To my mother and father

Contents

Pirate Gold

Just imagine . . .

It is midnight on a lonely island. Two men are digging on the sandy shore. One wears a gold earring and a red bandanna. The other man has a patch over his eye. Both are armed with swords and guns. They are pirates.

Slowly they lower a heavy wooden chest into a deep hole. The chest is heavy because it is full of gold and jewels. The pirates shovel sand into the hole. After they are finished, no one would guess that treasure is buried in this place. The pirates leave quickly.

They never return.

Is this a true story? Maybe. Treasure hunters are sure that pirates buried stolen gold in secret places all over the world. And they believe that lots of pirate treasure is still waiting for someone to discover it.

Pirates sailed the seas hundreds of years ago. They attacked ships with rich cargoes—ships full of gold and jewels. They took everything they wanted. Pirates didn't get any regular pay.

Each man got a share of what was found on a captured ship. So the more treasure on board the better.

Pirates were always ready for a fight. But they liked it better if sailors gave up without a battle. So they tried to scare them. Pirates flew a flag called the Jolly Roger. It wasn't jolly. It was usually black with a white skull on it. Sometimes it had an hourglass on it too. That meant "Your time is running out!"

A pirate flag.

One pirate scared everybody—even other pirates. He was a giant of a man. He had wild eyes. He wore six guns, two sharp curved swords, and two or three daggers. His real name was Edward Teach or Thatch—nobody knows for sure. But everybody called him Blackbeard. He liked to tie red ribbons in his long scraggly beard. One time he even tied burning candles in it. But the whole thing caught fire. He never did that again!

Blackbeard was as scary as he looked. Once, for no reason at all, he shot a friend. Blackbeard explained it this way: "If I don't shoot somebody now and then, people will forget who I am."

Blackbeard sailed the seas in the early 1700s. He attacked ships up and down the coast of North America. He is said to have buried lots of treasure. The stories usually add that he buried a headless skeleton along with his gold. Some people say that Blackbeard hid his loot on the

Isles of Shoals, off the coast of New Hampshire. Others say he buried it off the coast of North Carolina or Georgia. But nothing much has been found. Blackbeard didn't leave many clues. He always said, "Only the Devil and me knows where my gold is hid."

There are many other stories of pirate treasure. Cocos Island, off Central America, has even been nicknamed "Treasure Island." Has treasure been found there? No. But almost 500 separate groups of people have gone to Cocos to look for treasure! Why so many? Because stories say that four or five different pirates buried gold somewhere on the island.

Many pirates really did visit one special island. But not to hide their gold. To spend it.

They went to the town of Port Royal on the island of Jamaica. In the 1600s, Port Royal was called "the wickedest city in the world." Pirates from all over met there. They came in their

A True and Perfect Relation of that most Sad and Terrible

EARTHQUAKE, at Port-Royal in JAMAICA,

Which happened on *Tuesday* the 7th. of *June*, 1692.

Where, in Two Minutes time the Town was Sunk under Ground, and Two Thousand Souls Perished: With the manner of it at Large; in a Letter from thence, Written by Captain *Crocket*: As also of the *Earthquake* which happen'd in *England, Holland, Flanders, France, Germany, Zealand, &c.* And in most Parts of *Europe*: On *Thursday* the 8th of *September.* Being a Dreadful Warning to the Sleepy World: Or, God's heavy Judgments shewed on a Sinful People, as a Fore-runner of the Terrible Day of the Lord.

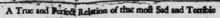

The EXPLANATION.

A. *The Houses Falling.* B. *The Churches.* C. *The Sugar-Works.* D. *The Mills.* E. *Tve Bridge in the whole Country.* F. *The Rock and Mountains.* G. *Captain Roden's House Sunk first into the Earth, with his Wife, and Family.* H. *The Ground rolling under the Monster's Feet.* I. *The great Church half Frost Sinking.* K. *The Earth Opening and Swallowing Multitudes of People on Morgan's Fort.* L. *The Minister Kneeling down in a Ring, with his People in the midst of the Earthquake in France.* M. *The Wharf covered with the Sea.* N. *Dr. Heath going from Ship to Ship to Visit the bruised People, and do his last Office to the dead Corpses that lay Floating from the Point.* O. *Thieves Robbing and Breaking open both Dwelling Houses and Ware-Houses during the Earthquake.* P. *Dr. Trapham, a Doctor of Physick, hanging by the Hands on a Rock of the Chimney, and one of his Children hanging about his Neck seeing his Wife and the rest of his Children a Sinking.* Q. *A Boat coming to save them.* K. *The Minister Preaching on a Tent to the People.* S. *The dead Bodies of some Hundreds floating about the Harbour.* T. *The Sea washing the dead Carkasses out of their Graves and Tombs, and dashed to pieces by the Earthquake.* V. *People swallow'd up in the Earth, several as high as their Necks with their Heads above Ground.* W. *The Dogs eating of Dead Mens Heads.* X. *Several Ships Cast away and driven into the very Town.* Y. *A Woman and her two Daughters beat to pieces one against the other.* Z. *Mr. Beckford his Diging out of the Ground.*

An old print of the earthquake at Port Royal.

fanciest clothes—leather boots, bright silk sashes, gold bracelets, and armbands. They came to gamble. They came to fight. They came to get drunk on one of their favorite drinks—rum and gunpowder.

Then, in just a few minutes, Port Royal changed forever. It happened on the morning of June 7, 1692. Suddenly, houses began to shake. People

ran outside crying "Earthquake!" The streets started to rise like waves in the sea. Great cracks opened in the ground. Men and women were swallowed up. Buildings crumbled and fell. Then a huge wave, taller than the tallest building, swept over Port Royal. Most of the city and 2,000 people slid to the bottom of the sea.

Many years passed. People told strange stories about the lost city. They said there were rows of buildings standing on the sea bottom. Sunken streets paved with gold. Underwater taverns with skeletons sitting at the tables. And pirate treasure everywhere.

The stories weren't true. But many divers believed them. They tried to swim down to the sunken city. All they found was mud. The city was buried.

Then, in 1965, a famous diver came to Port Royal. His name was Robert Marx. He brought men and machines with him. He wanted to explore the sunken city and find out how life had been lived there.

His work was dangerous. There were sharks and stinging fish in the water. Once a huge winged fish called a manta ray swam by. It was 12 feet wide! It put its great wings around one diver. It hugged him. Then it swam off!

Soon Marx found the walls of the city. He

brought up clay smoking pipes, candlesticks, old rum bottles, a silver watch, and much more. He even found two buildings still standing. He was happy to discover so many clues about life in old Port Royal. Marx wasn't really looking for treasure. But he found it! He and his divers were exploring near the ruins of an old tavern. They found a few silver coins. Then thousands of them. Treasure from the pirate city!

Robert Marx (right) and one of his divers with treasure from Port Royal.

Treasure hunters were thrilled at the news. Many others came to search the ruins of Port Royal. But many more kept on exploring lonely little islands where nothing had been found yet. They still felt sure that somewhere, in a wooden chest, beneath a sandy beach, pirate gold was waiting.

Sunken Treasure

July 30, 1715. Eleven ships sailed slowly along the coast of Florida. They were heavy with silver and gold. About 2,000 sailors were on board. The ships had to take their treasure all the way back to Spain—about 5,000 miles away. The voyage would be full of danger. Pirates sailed the ocean. Hurricanes struck without warning. And the sea was full of reefs—hard jagged ridges hidden just underwater. If the bottom of a ship scraped against one, it would be torn open.

The sea was very still. The ships were barely moving. Then the sky grew dark. Rain began to fall. The winds howled and giant waves crashed down. The storm grew worse. Now the waves were like mountains. Men were swept overboard. Wood cracked. Sails tore. Tons of water poured down. The ships were pushed toward the reefs. One ship sank to the bottom. Then another and another.

Ten ships went down in the terrible storm. A thousand men died. A fortune in treasure was lost.

Almost 250 years later a man was walking along a Florida beach. His name was Kip Wagner. His job was building houses. He had moved to a nearby town to build a new motel.

Kip was looking for old silver coins. He had been looking for years. He had heard stories about Spanish coins turning up on the beach— pieces of eight that came from sunken treasure ships. When a friend finally showed him some pieces of eight, Kip was surprised. They weren't

round. They weren't shiny. They weren't anything like the coins in his pocket. They were oddly shaped and blackened by the sea. If he had seen one, he would never have bothered to pick it up.

Even knowing what to look for didn't help Kip. He never found anything. Sometimes he thought he never would.

Blackened pieces of eight from the sea bottom.

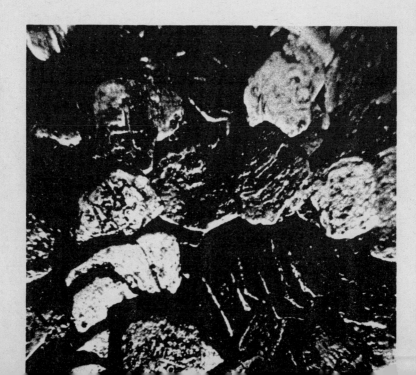

Pieces of eight after they've been cleaned and polished.

Kip used a metal detector. He would sweep the rod back and forth over the beach. If there was any metal under the sand, the detector would make a special noise. A beep.

Often the metal detector beeped. Kip would dig in the sand. And what would he find? A tin can.

Then one day the detector beeped the way it always did. Kip brushed away the sand. This time he saw a black, strangely shaped piece of metal. He couldn't believe it! An old silver coin! He had finally found one!

Kip picked it up. Pirates had killed for these coins. Treasure hunters had died trying to find them. And now he held one in his hand.

Kip decided something. He would never give up searching until he found a great treasure.

Kip went back to the same beach again and again. He found more silver coins, even some gold ones. He began to call the place his "money beach."

He had one big question. Where had all these coins come from? He felt sure they had washed up from the sea. Somewhere, probably nearby, was the wreck of a great treasure ship.

Kip swam out to look for the wreck. He cut himself on the sharp edges of the reefs. But he found nothing. He borrowed a boat. He cruised through the waves. He stared down into the water. Still nothing.

He was never going to find any treasure this way. He had to know where to look. He decided to stop searching in the ocean. Instead, he would search for answers in the library!

Kip had one important clue. The coins from the beach had dates on them. And no coin was dated later than 1715. He heard that some treasure ships had gone down in a hurricane in 1715. But no one knew where they had sunk.

Kip tried the biggest library in the country. The Library of Congress, in Washington, D.C. The library had a very rare book. It was 200 years old. Sure enough, it told about the shipwrecks of 1715! There was even a map! The map showed that the treasure ships had gone down within a few miles of his money beach!

Kip took to the ocean again. This time he made himself a special surfboard. He put a glass window in it. He could paddle along and see down into the water. Time after time Kip looked

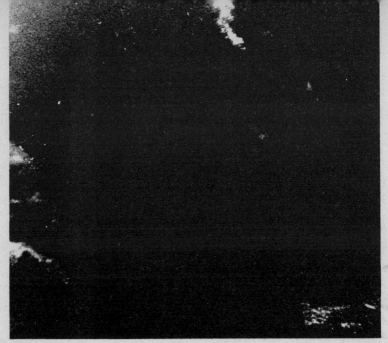

A cannon from a shipwreck.

for a wrecked ship beneath the waves.

Then one day he saw strange shapes. He paddled closer. They were cannons from a ship. Nearby was a huge anchor. Suddenly he knew. He had found the wreck! He had expected to see a whole ship lying on its side. But a wooden ship would be rotted away after almost 250 years in the ocean. Only the metal parts would last.

And the treasure? Kip was sure it was still there. But it must be scattered and buried under the sand.

Kip got special permission from the Florida government to search for treasure. He promised to give Florida part of any treasure he found. He bought an old boat and machines to move sand. He spent a year getting a team of eight men together. He liked and trusted every one of them. One morning, in January 1961, he set out for the wreck.

The team was excited. Kip was nervous. Storms made the sand at the bottom of the ocean move. What you could see one day might be covered up the next. Would he be able to find the wreck again?

The sea was rough. Kip had to steer the boat close to two dangerous reefs—the same reefs that had sunk the treasure ships.

The boat made it. The water was very cold.

Only two of the team had special diving suits to keep them warm. Down they went.

Then one diver broke through the water. He waved a handful of silver coins. "They're down there by the bushel!" he cried. He left the coins on the deck and disappeared. Then he was back, pushing what looked like a big black rock onto the ship. It was a mass of silver coins—all stuck together. There had to be a thousand of them!

Everyone began to laugh and shout "We're rich! We're rich!" And they all dived in! Nobody

cared how cold the water was! For the rest of the day they picked treasure off the bottom— some $80,000 worth.

And this was only the beginning. Later they found gold coins, jewelry, silver candlesticks. Their discoveries surprised the world. They found a gold chain $10\frac{1}{2}$ feet long! They found

The $10\frac{1}{2}$-foot-long gold chain with a dragon pendant.

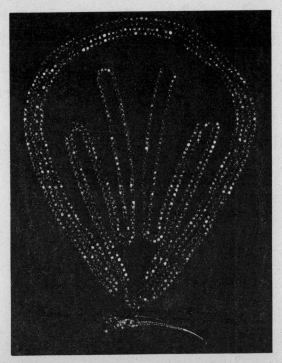

a wooden treasure chest. It was loaded with 3,000 coins. How had a wooden chest lasted after 250 years in the sea? No one could believe it. They found something even stranger—28 priceless cups and saucers from China. Not one was even cracked.

That wasn't all. Kip led his team to seven more treasure wrecks! They found more than $3 million in treasure!

Kip had made his dream come true. He was famous. Reporters followed him. He was invited all over the world. He was on television, in magazines. Treasure hunters everywhere tried to do what he had done.

And this was the man who thought he would never find even one silver coin!

The Dead King

Far away in the land of Egypt is a strange valley. It is lonely and silent. There are no trees. No grass or flowers. Just jagged cliffs, rocks, and sand. It is called the Valley of the Kings, and it belongs to the dead. Thousands of years ago the kings of Egypt were buried there—with fabulous treasures.

Many people hunted for the treasures. Howard Carter was one of them. He was an archeologist (ar-kee-AH-luh-jist). A scientist who digs in the earth for clues about the past. He came to Egypt in 1890 when he was only 17

years old. He learned all about the ancient Egyptians and the Valley of the Kings.

Long, long ago, when an Egyptian king died, he was buried with his best belongings. Why? The kings believed that, after death, their spirits went to another world. To be happy there, a king's spirit would need everything the king loved in life. Beautiful clothes. Fine furniture. Jewelry. Even food. The spirit would need a body, too. A body that would last forever. So the

Egyptians turned dead bodies into mummies.

The kings wanted to be sure that their mummies and their treasures would be safe. They put them into giant pyramids. But robbers broke into every one. So the kings decided to hide their burial places. They built secret tombs in the cliffs of the Valley of the Kings. They didn't know it, but their treasures still weren't safe.

For years every archeologist in Egypt dreamed of finding a king's tomb hidden in the valley.

Almost 30 tombs *were* found. But ancient robbers had always gotten there first. The treasures were gone.

By 1900 most archeologists had decided that there were no more kings' tombs left to find. Howard Carter thought they were wrong. He was sure that one king's tomb had never been discovered. The king's name was Tutankhamen (too-tonk-AH-mun). Sometimes he was called King Tut. He wasn't an important king. He ruled for just a short time. He died when he was only 18.

Howard met a man who agreed with him. He was a wealthy Englishman named Lord Carnarvon. They became partners. Lord Carnarvon gave Howard all the money he needed for his search. And in 1917 Howard began to dig in the valley.

For five long years Howard searched. He worked in burning heat, in terrible winds, and

Lord Carnarvon

in blinding dust storms. He found a few ancient
jars. But nothing more.

He was tired and discouraged. And Lord
Carnarvon wanted to give up. But Howard still
hoped. He had dug up some stone huts built in
ancient times. He had a feeling about them. He
asked Lord Carnarvon for one more chance.

When Howard went back to work, he brought a pet along. A yellow canary. His workmen called it the Golden Bird. They said it would bring them luck. Howard would make a discovery soon. And he did!

Howard and his workmen began to dig under the first hut. They found a step cut into the rocky ground! Then another and another. It was a hidden stairway! They cleared more rubble away. There was the top part of a door!

What was behind it? Could it be the entrance

to a king's tomb? Howard felt like breaking down the door. But he remembered all the years Lord Carnarvon had helped him. Howard wanted his friend to be there. It would take weeks for Carnarvon to come from England. But Howard decided to wait.

Howard waited and worried. Maybe it was a tomb—but an empty one. Maybe it wasn't a tomb at all! His workmen had their own worries. They were afraid of bad luck. Howard's canary had been eaten by a cobra! And a cobra was the sacred serpent of the kings of Egypt. The workmen were sure Howard had found a king's tomb. And now the king was angry!

Finally Lord Carnarvon arrived. Together he and Howard uncovered the bottom part of the door. Howard was amazed at what he saw. There was the royal seal of Tutankhamen! It was a king's tomb! At last he had found what he was looking for!

But there was still one question. Would it be empty?

They broke through the door. Behind it was a long passageway filled from floor to ceiling with small stones. It took many days to cart all the stones away. Then they came to another door.

Howard made a small hole in it. His hands were shaking. He held a candle up. At first he couldn't see into the darkness. Then, slowly, he

The golden chariot and other treasure in King Tut's tomb.

made out the shapes of statues and strange animals, and he saw gold. Gold everywhere! Lord Carnarvon was standing just behind him. "Can you see anything?" he asked. Howard could hardly speak. "Yes," he said. "Wonderful things!"

Howard made an opening in the door. Inside, the treasure seemed even more wonderful. There were golden couches carved with strange animals. Golden chariots. A chest full of jeweled robes and sandals. A golden throne.

A crowd waiting outside Tut's tomb.

And that was just one room! There were three other rooms too. All filled with treasure. King Tut's mummy rested in one of them. That was the rarest treasure of all.

The news of Howard's discovery spread around the world. Visitors poured into the valley. They came over the rocky paths on donkeys, in carts,

and in automobiles. They slept outside the tomb.
Carter posted an army of guards. And guards to
guard the guards.

Strangers wrote to him. They asked for a little
something from the tomb—maybe a gold bar.
Or they warned him that he was in danger.
There were evil spirits in the tomb!

Then, very suddenly, Lord Carnarvon died. Newspapers made up stories. They said he died because he went into the tomb. It was the mummy's revenge! They said there was a curse written on King Tut's coffin. And a deadly poison on the treasures. The truth was that Lord Carnarvon's death had been caused by an insect bite. He had been sick even before he came to Egypt. But that didn't stop the stories.

Howard missed his partner. But he wasn't afraid. He went back to the tomb to open King Tut's coffin. He was going to learn exactly how an Egyptian king was buried.

When he opened the coffin he found another inside! And then another. The third coffin was made of solid gold. More than 200 pounds of it. Slowly Carter raised the lid. And there was the mummy of the king. This was a special moment. Carter felt as though he were back in ancient Egypt. Back in the time of Tut.

Howard Carter (left) working on Tut's coffin.

It took Carter 10 years to empty the tomb. There were over 5,000 ancient treasures inside. Each one had to be treated with the greatest care. Carter kept a few of the treasures. The rest went to a museum in Egypt. He left Tut's body where it had rested for over 3,000 years. And do you know what? It is still there today.

In 1977 the Egyptian museum gave Americans a chance to see what Carter had found. They lent the treasures to some museums in the United States. People fought for tickets. They slept outside the museum to be sure of getting in. Millions of Americans saw the exhibit. They were able to imagine what it was like to discover the greatest ancient treasure ever found.

Some people remembered those stories about the mummy's curse. They were worried. But reporters pointed something out. Almost everyone who helped empty the tomb lived to be old. Even Howard Carter.

At least one person still had doubts. Lord Carnarvon's son was interviewed. Would he go into King Tut's tomb? reporters asked. "Not," he said, "for a million dollars."

The gold mask found on King Tut's mummy.

Treasure, Treasure Everywhere

How much treasure is still lost or buried? Billions of dollars' worth. In gold and silver and jewels! Treasure hunters all agree on this. Why so much? People have been hiding and losing treasure for thousands of years. It adds up!

Here are some famous stories about lost treasures still waiting to be found.

Sunken Treasure

Some of the biggest treasures are underwater. Hundreds of ships full of gold lie on the ocean bottom. There are treasure ships in lakes and rivers, too. One sunken treasure ship is in a very surprising place. It's on the bottom of one of the world's busiest harbors. Right off East 135th Street in New York City! And it's been there since 1780! The ship's name is the *Hussar*. It was sent from England with $2 million in silver and gold. The money was meant to pay British soldiers in America. The *Hussar's* anchor has been found. But no one has brought up the gold.

It sounds as if it would be so easy to get the treasure. But it is not. The *Hussar* went down in deep water. At the time the ship sank, treasure hunters didn't have inventions like diving suits to help them search the bottom. Today there are other problems. The ship has been underwater for over 200 years. So the wreck has probably rotted away. And the river bottom is made up of at least 15 feet of soft ooze and trash.

By now, experts say, the gold may be scattered along miles of the river. And buried in that ooze.

Even if nobody ever finds the *Hussar*, there are plenty of other ships to look for. There are stories of sunken treasure ships from all over the world. People say that there's a steamboat in the Mississippi River. It sank in 1871 with a fortune on board. There are treasure wrecks as far away as Japan and Australia. There's even a sunken treasure *train*! In 1876 the train plunged into a river in Ohio. One car held $2 million in gold bars.

Stolen Goods

Lots of treasure gets stolen. And there's a funny thing about robbers. They're scared of other robbers! So they often hide what they steal. Many outlaws of the Old West hid their loot. Jesse James is one of the most famous. He robbed stagecoaches, trains, and banks during the 1870s. But he was polite. He liked to pause when he was robbing somebody and introduce his gang members. Once the James Gang stole

Jesse James at age 17.

a million dollars in gold bars. People say Jesse buried it near Lawton, Oklahoma. He marked the spot with two axe heads and a bucket. But before he could go back for it, he was killed. As far as anybody knows, the treasure is still there. Somewhere.

Pirate Treasure

There were many other famous pirates besides Blackbeard. Many are said to have buried treasure.

Sometimes when pirates were caught, they told where the buried treasure was. Once there was a pirate named Charles Wilson. Right before he was hanged, he gave directions to his treasure. He named an island in Maryland and said, "Ye treasure lies hidden in a clump of trees near three creeks lying a hundred paces or more north of the second inlet." People rushed to the island. But no one found the treasure.

Hidden Tombs

The Egyptians weren't the only people who buried their dead with treasure. Hidden tombs full of gold and jewels have been found all over the world. The biggest tomb was found in China. It just looked like a big grassy hill covered with trees. But in 1974 some men started to dig a well. And they found the burial place of an em-

Part of the clay army from the Chinese emperor's tomb.

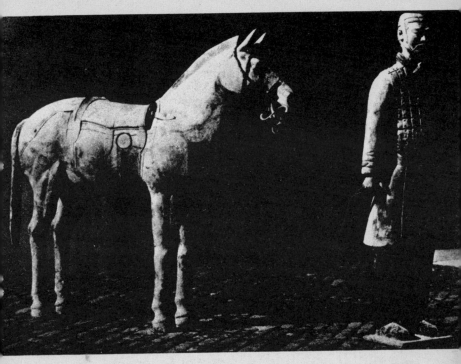

Two of the life-size clay figures.

peror! The tomb went on for miles. It was over 2,000 years old. Inside was treasure and an army of thousands of life-size clay people, horses, and chariots. Archeologists believe that many other hidden tombs are yet to be found. Tombs of kings and queens and nobles buried long, long ago.

War Loot

Lots of people hide treasure in wartime so that the enemy can't take it. Sometimes they get killed. Sometimes they forget where the treasure is. So the treasure stays where it was hidden.

Lots of treasure gets stolen in wartime too. During World War II, Hitler and his men stole gold and jewels and paintings and statues from many countries. After the fighting was over, people tried to find Hitler's stolen treasure. And they did! It was hidden in secret caves, old mines, and castles all over Germany. But did they find it all? Many treasure hunters say no. It's still there waiting to be found.

Lost Mines

How do you lose a gold mine? It must be easy, because treasure hunters tell lots of stories about gold mines that were found and then lost.

One famous story is about the Lost Breyfogle Mine. It is named for the man who found it and lost it—Jacob Breyfogle. Around 1865 he was trying to cross a desert in California called Death Valley. His horse died. He ran out of food and water. He had to live on bugs, roots, and herbs. But he kept going. Suddenly he saw a rich vein of gold and silver in some pink rocks. He took all he could fit in his pack. He carried it until he finally made it to a town. Then he tried to go back to the place that would make him rich. It was no use. He never did find the spot. But every year treasure hunters go to Death Valley to try their luck.

Then there's the Lost Dutchman Mine. The story goes like this. In the 1870s a man called the Dutchman found gold in the Arizona mountains. He brought out sacks of nuggets. He bragged about his mine. But he wouldn't tell anyone where it was. Different men tried to trail him. None were seen again. After the Dutchman died, thousands more people tried to find the mine. A few of them were found murdered. It is said there's an Indian curse on the mine. Or that an old miner shoots anyone who comes near. One thing is sure. The Lost Dutchman Mine is still lost.

Treasure, Treasure Anywhere

Treasure may be hidden anywhere. On a mountaintop. In a swamp. Even in the middle of a busy city. Once a woman moved into a new apartment in New York. She defrosted her refrigerator. When the ice melted, she found a dozen thousand-dollar bills taped inside the freezer! In 1926 two teenagers were plowing a field in Tennessee. A gold coin gleamed in the soil. And another. Soon they had a whole jar full!

Nobody was even looking for these treasures. Nobody told any stories about them. They were a big surprise! And sometime, maybe even today, someone will find another hidden treasure. It could be a pirate chest. Or a king's crown. Or a strange, wonderful treasure like nothing that has ever been discovered before. Who can tell? There are so many hidden treasures to find!

About the Author and Illustrator

Judy Donnelly remembers reading *Treasure Island* when she was about eight years old and scouring her Connecticut neighborhood for treasure—with no luck whatsoever. Today her treasure hunting is confined mostly to garage sales, but she still dreams of turning up a few gold doubloons or some pieces of eight.

Ms. Donnelly is a children's book editor at a New York publishing house. A graduate of Barnard College, she lives in Manhattan with her husband and twin daughters. This is her first book for children.

Charles Robinson has illustrated more than twenty-five children's books, including several in the popular Soup series (*Soup on Wheels, Soup's Drum*) published by Knopf. The father of three grown children, Mr. Robinson lives in Mendham, New Jersey, with his wife.

Key

Lost Treasure in the United States

This map shows just some of the lost treasures said to be in the United States. The stories of treasures 1 to 10 are told in this book.